Rules at School

Sharon Coan, M.S.Ed.

We have **rules** at school.

Rules help us get along.

Rules help us **learn**.

Our teacher writes
the rules.

We follow the rules.

We stand in line.

We raise our hands.

blue
purple
brown
black
WORD WALL
pal – pail
hop – hope
Tim – time
pet – Pete
cut – cute

We listen.

We take turns.

We **share.**

We use our inside voices.

We walk inside.

We help each other.

We have rules at school.

Rules help us get along.

Rules help us learn.

Write It!

1. Think about the rules at your school.
2. Write two school rules.

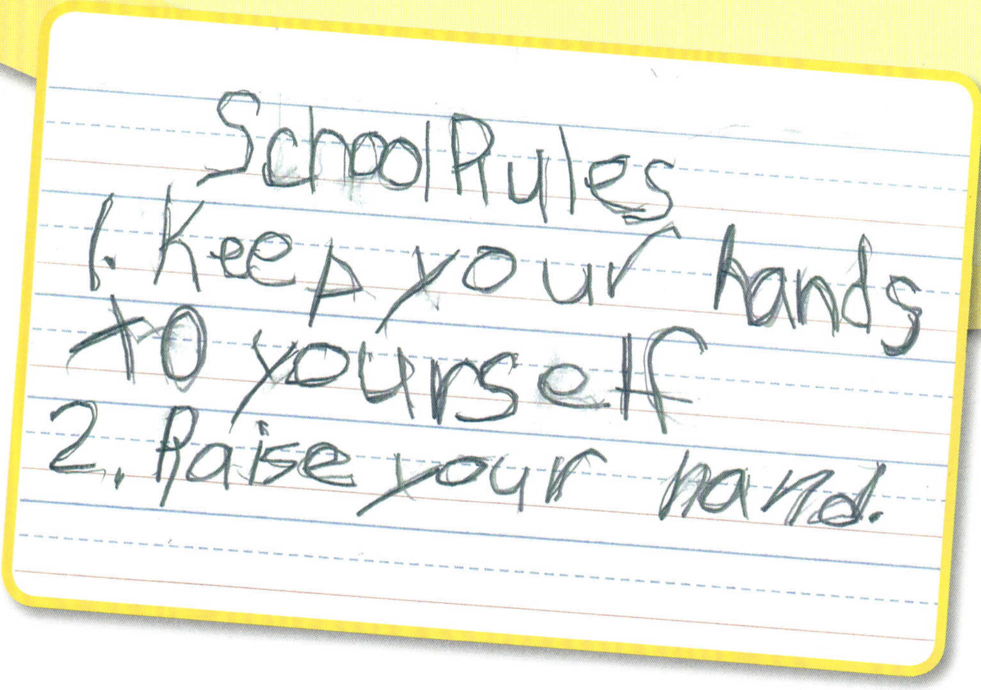

3. Talk about the rules with a friend.

Glossary

learn—to find out and know something

rules—things that tell you what you may or may not do

share—to use things with other people

Index

Your Turn!

There are rules at school. What happens when you follow the rules? Draw a picture.

Consultants

Shelley Scudder
Gifted Teacher
Broward County Schools

Caryn Williams, M.S.Ed.
Madison County Schools
Huntsville, AL

Publishing Credits

Conni Medina, M.A.Ed., *Managing Editor*
Lee Aucoin, *Creative Director*
Torrey Maloof, *Editor*
Lexa Hoang, *Designer*
Stephanie Reid, *Photo Editor*
Rachelle Cracchiolo, M.S.Ed., *Publisher*

Image Credits: Cover, p.1 Blend Images/Ariel Skelley/Getty Images; pp.5, 12–13 Jim West/Alamy; pp.6, 9 Myrleen Pearson/Alamy; p.4 Richard Dickin/Associated Press; p.7 Dave Nagel/Getty Iamges; pp.16–17 Juan Silva/Getty Images; p.8 Tim Platt/Getty Images; Backcover, p.2 Lexa Hoang; p.18 track5/iStockphoto; p.11 taylorg/iStockphoto; p.24 quavondo/iStockphoto; p.22 Christopher Futcher/iStockphoto; p.23 (top) ktaylorg/iStockphoto; p.10 CEFutcher/iStockphoto; p.14 kali9/iStockphoto; p.23 (bottom) CEFutcher/iStockphoto; p.19 Teacher Created Materials; All other images from Shutterstock.

Teacher Created Materials
5301 Oceanus Drive
Huntington Beach, CA 92649-1030
http://www.tcmpub.com

ISBN 978-1-4333-7343-5

Printed by: 590835
Printed in: China